Cocktails and Mocktails

Publications International, Ltd.

Louis Weber, CEO
Publications International, Ltd.
8140 Lehigh Ave
Morton Grove, IL 60053

ISBN: 978-1-63938-944-5

Manufactured in China.

8 7 6 5 4 3 2 1

WARNING: Food preparation, baking and cooking involve inherent dangers: misuse of electric products, sharp electric tools, boiling water, hot stoves, allergic reactions, foodborne illnesses and the like, pose numerous potential risks. Publications International, Ltd. (PIL) assumes no responsibility or liability for any damages you may experience as a result of following recipes, instructions, tips or advice in this publication.

While we hope this publication helps you find new ways to eat delicious foods, you may not always achieve the results desired due to variations in ingredients, cooking temperatures, typos, errors, omissions, or individual cooking abilities.

According to the Surgeon General, women should not drink alcoholic beverages during pregnancy because of the risk of birth defects. Consumption of alcoholic beverages impairs your ability to drive a car or operate machinery and may cause health problems. If you drink, do not drive.

Contents

Classic Cocktails

Mojito

MAKES 2 SERVINGS

- **8 fresh mint leaves, plus additional sprigs for garnish**
- **2 ounces lime juice**
- **2 teaspoons superfine sugar or powdered sugar**
- **3 ounces light rum**
- **Chilled club soda or seltzer**
- **2 lime slices**

Combine four mint leaves, lime juice and sugar in each of two highball glasses; mash with wooden spoon or muddler. Fill glasses with ice. Pour rum over ice; top with club soda. Garnish with lime slices and additional mint leaves.

Tequila Sour

MAKES 1 SERVING

2 ounces tequila

1 ounce lemon juice

2 teaspoons simple syrup (recipe follows)

2 dashes bitters

Maraschino cherry

Fill cocktail shaker half full with ice; add tequila, lemon juice, simple syrup and bitters in cocktail shaker. Shake 30 seconds or until very cold; strain into glass. Garnish with cherry.

Simple Syrup

Combine 1 cup water and 1 cup sugar in small saucepan. Cook over medium heat just until sugar is dissolved, stirring frequently. Cool to room temperature; store syrup in glass jar in refrigerator.

Ramos Gin Fizz

MAKES 1 SERVING

2 ounces gin

1 ounce whipping cream

½ ounce lemon juice

½ ounce lime juice

1 teaspoon superfine sugar

2 dashes orange flower water

1 egg white

Chilled club soda

Combine gin, cream, lemon juice, lime juice, sugar, orange flower water and egg white in cocktail shaker; shake without ice 30 seconds. Add 1 cup ice cubes to shaker; shake 30 seconds or until very cold. Strain into chilled highball or Collins glass; top with club soda.

Note

A Ramos Gin Fizz is typically not served over ice, but if you don't have a chilled glass, adding a few ice cubes will help keep the drink cold longer (although it will also dilute the drink).

French Connection >

MAKES 1 SERVING

1½ ounces cognac

¾ ounce amaretto

Pour cognac and amaretto over ice in old fashioned glass; stir until blended.

French Connection No. 2

Substitute orange liqueur for the amaretto.

Old Fashioned

MAKES 1 SERVING

1 sugar cube

2 dashes Angostura bitters

1 teaspoon water

2 ounces whiskey

Lemon peel twist

Place sugar cube, bitters and water in old fashioned glass; muddle until sugar is dissolved. Fill glass half full with ice; stir in whiskey and lemon twist.

Grapefruit Daiquiri >

MAKES 1 SERVING

¼ cup grapefruit juice
2 ounces light rum
½ ounce lime juice
1 teaspoon maraschino cherry juice
Lime slice

Fill cocktail shaker half full with ice; add grapefruit juice, rum, lime juice and maraschino cherry juice. Shake 30 seconds or until very cold; strain into cocktail glass. Garnish with lime slice.

Moonwalk

MAKES 1 SERVING

1 ounce grapefruit juice
1 ounce orange liqueur
3 drops rosewater*
Chilled champagne or sparkling wine

Rosewater can be found at many liquor stores and supermarkets as well as Middle Eastern grocery stores.

Fill cocktail shaker half full with ice; add grapefruit juice, liqueur and rosewater. Shake 30 seconds or until very cold; strain into champagne flute. Top with champagne.

Rusty Nail >

MAKES 1 SERVING

1½ ounces Scotch

1 ounce Drambuie

Lemon wedge

Pour Scotch and Drambuie over ice in old fashioned glass; stir until blended. Garnish with lemon.

Hunter's Cocktail

MAKES 1 SERVING

1½ ounces whiskey

½ ounce cherry brandy

Pour whiskey and brandy over ice in old fashioned glass; stir until blended.

Champagne Cocktail

MAKES 1 SERVING

1½ ounces brandy

1 ounce orange liqueur

8 ounces chilled champagne

Place brandy and liqueur in wine glass; top with champagne.

Classic Margarita

MAKES 2 SERVINGS

Lime wedges
Coarse salt
4 ounces tequila
2 ounces orange liqueur
2 ounces lime juice
Lime slices or wedges

1. Rub rims of two margarita glasses with lime wedges; dip in salt.

2. Fill cocktail shaker half full with ice; add tequila, liqueur and lime juice. Shake 30 seconds or until very cold; strain into glasses. Garnish with lime slices.

Frozen Margarita

Rub rim of two margarita glasses with lime wedges; dip in salt. Combine tequila, orange liqueur, lime juice and 2 cups ice in blender; blend until smooth. Pour into glasses; garnish with lime slices.

White Russian >

MAKES 1 SERVING

- **1½ ounces vodka**
- **1 ounce coffee liqueur**
- **1 ounce whipping cream**

Fill cocktail shaker half full with ice; add vodka and liqueur. Stir or shake 30 seconds or until very cold; strain into ice-filled glass. Top with cream; gently swirl. Or add cream to cocktail shaker; shake until very cold. Strain into ice-filled glass.

French 75

MAKES 1 SERVING

- **2 ounces gin**
- **½ ounce lemon juice**
- **1 teaspoon superfine sugar**
- **2 ounces chilled champagne or sparkling wine**

Fill cocktail shaker half full with ice; add gin, lemon juice and sugar. Shake 30 seconds or until very cold; strain into champagne flute or coupe. Top with champagne; stir gently.

Sidecar >

MAKES 1 SERVING

2 ounces brandy or cognac

2 ounces orange liqueur

½ ounce lemon juice

Orange twist

Fill cocktail shaker half full with ice; add brandy, liqueur and lemon juice. Shake 30 seconds or until very cold; strain into coupe or cocktail glass. Garnish with orange twist.

Boulevardier

MAKES 1 SERVING

1½ ounces bourbon

1 ounce sweet vermouth

1 ounce Campari

Orange slice or twist

Fill mixing glass or cocktail shaker half full with ice; add bourbon, vermouth and Campari. Stir 30 seconds or until cold; strain into old fashioned glass. Garnish with orange slice.

Martini Madness

West Side

MAKES 1 SERVING

- 2 ounces lemon vodka
- 1 ounce lemon juice
- ½ ounce simple syrup (page 6)
- 1 fresh mint sprig
- Chilled club soda

Fill cocktail shaker half full with ice; add vodka, lemon juice, simple syrup and mint. Shake 30 seconds or until very cold. Top with splash of club soda; strain into chilled coupe or cocktail glass.

Espresso Martini >

MAKES 1 SERVING

- **2 ounces vodka**
- **1 ounce brewed espresso, cooled or cold brew concentrate**
- **¾ ounce coffee liqueur**
- **½ ounce simple syrup (page 6; optional)**

Fill cocktail shaker half full with ice; add vodka, espresso, liqueur and simple syrup, if desired. Shake 30 seconds or until very cold; strain into coupe or cocktail glass.

Vesper

MAKES 1 SERVING

- **3 ounces gin**
- **1 ounce vodka**
- **½ ounce Lillet Blanc**
- **Lemon twist**

Fill cocktail shaker half full with ice; add gin, vodka and Lillet Blanc. Shake 30 seconds or until very cold; strain into cocktail glass. Garnish with lemon twist.

Martinez >

MAKES 1 SERVING

1½ ounces gin

¾ ounce sweet vermouth

½ ounce maraschino liqueur

2 dashes orange bitters

Lemon or orange peel twist

Fill cocktail shaker half full with ice; add gin, vermouth, liqueur and bitters. Shake 30 seconds or until very cold; strain into coupe or cocktail glass. Garnish with lemon twist.

Classic Dry Martini

MAKES 1 SERVING

2 ounces gin or vodka

1½ teaspoons dry vermouth

Fill cocktail shaker half full with ice; add gin and vermouth. Stir 30 seconds or until very cold; strain into chilled cocktail glass.

Lemon Drop >

MAKES 1 SERVING

- 2 ounces vodka
- ¾ ounce lemon juice
- ½ ounce simple syrup (page 6)
- Lemon slice

Fill cocktail shaker half full with ice; add vodka, lemon juice and simple syrup. Shake 30 seconds or until very cold; strain into cocktail glass. Garnish with lemon slice.

Cosmopolitan

MAKES 1 SERVING

- 2 ounces lemon vodka
- 1 ounce orange liqueur
- 1 ounce cranberry juice
- ½ ounce lime juice
- Lime wedge

Fill cocktail shaker half full with ice; add vodka, orange liqueur and juices. Shake 30 seconds or until very cold; strain into cocktail glass. Garnish with lime wedge.

Apple Martini >

MAKES 1 SERVING

- **2 ounces vodka**
- **1 ounce apple schnapps**
- **1 ounce apple juice**
- **Apple slices**

Fill cocktail shaker half full with ice; add vodka, schnapps and apple juice. Shake 30 seconds or until very cold; strain into cocktail glass. Garnish with apple slices.

Sour Apple Martini

Substitute sour apple schnapps for apple schnapps.

Clover Club

MAKES 1 SERVING

- **1½ ounces gin**
- **¾ ounce lemon juice**
- **½ ounce dry vermouth**
- **2 teaspoons grenadine or raspberry syrup**
- **1 egg white**

Combine gin, lemon juice, vermouth, grenadine and egg white in cocktail shaker; shake 10 seconds without ice. Fill shaker half full with ice; shake about 30 seconds or until very cold. Strain into cocktail glass.

Kamikaze >

MAKES 1 SERVING

1 ounce vodka

1 ounce orange liqueur

1 ounce lime juice

Lime slice

Fill cocktail shaker half full with ice; add vodka, liqueur and lime juice. Shake 30 seconds or until very cold; strain into cocktail glass. Garnish with lime slice.

Melon Ball

MAKES 1 SERVING

3 ounces orange or pineapple juice

2 ounces melon-flavored liqueur

1 ounce vodka

Fill cocktail shaker half full with ice; add orange juice, liqueur and vodka. Shake 30 seconds or until very cold; strain into cocktail glass.

French Martini >

MAKES 1 SERVING

- **2 ounces vodka**
- **2 ounces pineapple juice**
- **½ ounce raspberry liqueur**
- **Fresh raspberries**

Fill cocktail shaker half full with ice; add vodka, pineapple juice and liqueur. Shake 30 seconds or until very cold; strain into cocktail glass. Garnish with raspberries.

Chocolate Martini

MAKES 1 SERVING

- **2 ounces vodka or vanilla vodka**
- **1½ ounces crème de cacao**
- **Chocolate shavings**

Fill cocktail shaker half full with ice; add vodka and crème de cacao. Shake 30 seconds or until very cold; strain into cocktail glass. Garnish with chocolate shavings.

Mint Chocolate Martini

Add ½ ounce crème de menthe to cocktail shaker.

Tropical Treats

Sea Breeze

MAKES 1 SERVING

- **3 ounces cranberry juice**
- **2 ounces grapefruit juice**
- **1½ ounces vodka**
- **Grapefruit wedge**

Fill cocktail shaker half full with ice; add cranberry juice, grapefruit juice and vodka. Stir 30 seconds or until very cold; strain into ice-filled Collins or highball glass. Garnish with grapefruit wedge.

Tequila Sunrise >

MAKES 1 SERVING

6 ounces orange juice
2 ounces tequila
½ ounce grenadine
Orange slice and maraschino cherry

Fill cocktail shaker half full with ice; add tequila and orange juice. Shake 30 seconds or until very cold; strain into hurricane glass. Pour in grenadine; let sink to bottom of glass. (Do not stir.) Garnish with orange slice and cherry.

Hurricane

MAKES 1 SERVING

2 ounces light rum
2 ounces dark rum
1 ounce passion fruit juice
1 ounce orange juice
1 ounce lime juice
½ ounce grenadine (optional)
Lime slices

Fill cocktail shaker half full with ice; add rums, juices and grenadine, if desired. Shake until blended; strain into ice-filled hurricane glass. Garnish with lime slices.

Blue Hawaii

MAKES 1 SERVING

- **3 ounces pineapple juice**
- **1 ounce vodka**
- **1 ounce light rum**
- **1 ounce sour mix, bottled or homemade (recipe follows)**
- **½ ounce blue curaçao**
- **Pineapple slice**

Fill cocktail shaker half full with ice; add pineapple juice, vodka, rum, sour mix and curaçao. Shake until blended; strain into ice-filled hurricane glass. Garnish with pineapple wedge.

Sour Mix

Combine 1 cup water and 1 cup sugar in small saucepan. Cook over medium heat just until sugar is dissolved, stirring frequently. Pour into glass jar; stir in 1 cup lemon juice and ½ cup lime juice. Cool completely; store in refrigerator.

Blue Hawaiian

Omit sour mix and add 1 ounce cream of coconut and 1 teaspoon sugar to cocktail shaker.

Zombie

MAKES 1 SERVING

- 2 ounces light rum
- 1 ounce dark rum
- 1 ounce lime juice
- 1 ounce pineapple juice
- 1 ounce orange juice or papaya juice
- ½ ounce apricot brandy
- 1 teaspoon sugar or simple syrup (page 6)
- ½ ounce 151-proof rum
- ½ ounce grenadine
- Fresh mint sprig

Fill cocktail shaker half full with ice; add rums, lime juice, pineapple juice, orange juice, brandy and sugar. Shake 30 seconds or until very cold; strain into Collins glass filled with crushed ice. Float 151-proof rum and grenadine on top. Garnish with mint.

Blended Variation

Combine light rum, dark rum, lime juice, pineapple juice, orange juice, brandy, sugar and ½ cup ice in blender; blend until smooth. Pour mixture into Collins or highball glass. Float 151-proof rum and grenadine on top.

Paloma >

MAKES 1 SERVING

- 1 grapefruit slice
- Coarse salt
- 2 ounces grapefruit juice
- ½ ounce lime juice
- 1 teaspoon sugar
- 2 ounces tequila
- 2 ounces club soda
- Fresh rosemary sprig

Rub rim of old fashioned glass with grapefruit slice; dip in coarse salt. Combine grapefruit juice, lime juice and sugar in glass; stir until sugar is dissolved. Fill glass with ice; stir in tequila and top with club soda. Garnish with rosemary sprig and grapefruit slice.

Don Pedro

MAKES 1 SERVING

- 1 cup vanilla ice cream
- 2 ounces whipping cream
- 1 ounce whiskey
- 1 ounce coffee liqueur

Combine ice cream, cream, whiskey and liqueur in blender; blend until smooth. Serve in hurricane glass.

Tropical Pineapple Daiquiri >

MAKES 4 SERVINGS

- ½ **pineapple, peeled, cored and cut into pieces**
- 1 **small mango, peeled and cut into pieces**
- 6 **ounces coconut rum**
- 8 **fresh mint leaves**
- **Pineapple wedges and/or additional fresh mint**

Combine ice, pineapple, mango, rum and 8 mint leaves in blender; blend until smooth. Pour into ice-filled glasses. Garnish with pineapple wedge and additional mint.

Piña Colada

MAKES 1 SERVING

- 4 **ounces pineapple juice**
- 1½ **ounces light rum**
- 1½ **ounces coconut cream**
- ½ **cup crushed ice**
- **Pineapple wedge and maraschino cherry**

Combine pineapple juice, rum and coconut cream in blender. Add ice; blend until smooth. Pour into Collins or hurricane glass; garnish with pineapple wedge and cherry.

Coco Loco >

MAKES 1 SERVING

- 4 ounces pineapple juice
- 2 ounces light rum
- 1 ounce cream of coconut
- 1 ounce milk
- ½ ounce amaretto
- 1 teaspoon grenadine
- ½ cup ice cubes
- Pineapple wedge

Combine pineapple juice, rum, cream of coconut, milk, amaretto, grenadine and ice in blender; blend until smooth. Serve in wine glass. Garnish with pineapple wedge.

Daiquiri

MAKES 1 SERVING

- 1½ ounces light rum
- ¾ ounce lime juice
- ¼ ounce simple syrup (page 6) *or* 1 teaspoon powdered sugar
- Lime wedge

Fill cocktail shaker half full with ice; add rum, lime juice and simple syrup. Shake 30 seconds or until very cold; strain into cocktail glass or margarita glass. Garnish with lime wedge.

Jungle Bird >

MAKES 1 SERVING

- **1½ ounces Jamaican or dark aged rum**
- **1½ ounces pineapple juice**
- **¾ ounce Campari**
- **½ ounce lime juice**
- **½ ounce simple syrup (page 6)**
- **Pineapple wedge**

Fill cocktail shaker with ice; add rum, pineapple juice, Campari, lime juice and simple syrup. Shake 30 seconds or until very cold; strain into ice-filled old fashioned glass. Garnish with pineapple wedge.

Mai Tai

MAKES 1 SERVING

- **1 ounce light rum**
- **1 ounce orange liqueur**
- **½ ounce grenadine**
- **½ ounce orgeat syrup***
- **½ ounce lime juice**
- **1 ounce dark rum**

Almond-flavored syrup.

Fill cocktail shaker half full with ice; add light rum, liqueur, grenadine, orgeat syrup and lime juice. Shake 30 seconds or until very cold; strain into old fashioned glass. Pour dark rum over top (do not stir).

Singapore Sling >

MAKES 1 SERVING

4 ounces pineapple juice
1 ounce gin
½ ounce lime juice
½ ounce cherry liqueur
½ ounce grenadine
¼ ounce orange liqueur
¼ ounce Bénédictine
Dash of bitters
Maraschino cherry and pineapple wedge

Fill cocktail shaker half full with ice; add pineapple juice, gin, lime juice, cherry liqueur, grenadine, orange liqueur, Bénédictine and bitters. Shake 30 seconds or until very cold; strain into ice-filled highball glass. Garnish with cherry and pineapple.

Painkiller

MAKES 1 SERVING

4 ounces pineapple juice
2 ounces orange juice
2 ounces dark rum
1 ounce cream of coconut
Freshly grated nutmeg

Combine pineapple juice, orange juice, rum and cream of coconut in ice-filled hurricane glass. Stir until blended. Sprinkle with nutmeg.

Low-ABV Sippers

Bicicletta

MAKES 1 SERVING

3 ounces dry white wine
2 ounces Campari
Chilled club soda or soda water
Fresh thyme sprigs

Fill old fashioned glass with ice; add wine and Campari. Fill with club soda; stir gently to mix. Garnish with thyme sprigs.

Negroni Sbagliato >

MAKES 1 SERVING

1 ounce sweet vermouth

1 ounce Campari

1 ounce chilled prosecco

Fill old fashioned glass with ice; add vermouth and Campari. Top with prosecco; stir gently.

Ranch Water

MAKES 1 SERVING

2 ounces tequila

1½ ounces lime juice

6 ounces chilled sparkling mineral water

Fill tall glass with ice. Add tequila and lime juice; stir to blend. Top with sparkling water.

Sherry Cobbler >

MAKES 1 SERVING

- ½ **teaspoon orange liqueur**
- ½ **teaspoon simple syrup (page 6)**
- 4 **ounces dry sherry (amontillado or oloroso)**
- **Orange slice**

Fill large wine glass or old fashioned glass half full with crushed ice. Add liqueur and simple syrup; stir until blended. Stir in sherry; garnish with orange slice.

Shandy

MAKES 1 SERVING

- 6 **ounces chilled beer**
- 6 **ounces chilled carbonated lemonade, lemon-lime soda, ginger beer or ginger ale**
- **Lemon slice**

Pour beer into chilled large wine glass or pint glass; top with lemonade. Garnish with lemon slice.

Apple Cider Mimosa >

MAKES 1 SERVING

3 ounces chilled apple cider (nonalcoholic)

3 ounces chilled champagne

Apple slice

Pour cider into champagne flute; top with champagne. Garnish with apple slice.

Calimocho

MAKES 1 SERVING

3 ounces red wine

3 ounces chilled cola

Lemon wedge

Pour wine and cola over ice in tall glass or wine glass. Garnish with lemon wedge.

Cuban Beer Spritzer >

MAKES 4 TO 6 SERVINGS

- **3 cups (24 ounces) chilled beer (pilsner or pale ale)**
- **3 cups (24 ounces) chilled ginger ale**
- **4 ounces lime juice**
- **⅓ cup sugar**
- **2 cups crushed ice**
- **Lime slices**

Combine beer, ginger ale, lime juice and sugar in large pitcher; stir until sugar dissolves. Divide ice among glasses; pour spritzer over ice. Garnish with lime slices.

Grapefruit Radler

MAKES 1 SERVING

- **4 ounces grapefruit juice**
- **1 teaspoon sugar**
- **1 bottle (12 ounces) cold wheat beer**
- **Cold grapefruit seltzer soda or water (optional)**

Combine grapefruit juice and sugar in large glass; stir to dissolve sugar. Add beer; stir gently to mix. Top with soda, if desired.

Bellini >

MAKES 1 SERVING

3 ounces peach nectar*

4 ounces chilled champagne or dry sparkling wine

**Or peel and pit a ripe medium peach and purée in blender.*

Pour peach nectar into chilled champagne flute; slowly pour in champagne.

Hawaiian Mimosa

MAKES 1 SERVING

4 ounces chilled sparkling wine, champagne or prosecco

2 ounces chilled pineapple juice

1½ ounces coconut rum

½ ounce grenadine

Orange slice

Layer sparkling wine, pineapple juice and rum in wine glass or champagne flute. Slowly pour in grenadine; do not stir. Garnish with orange slice.

Marvelous Mocktails

Lemon and Pomegranate Spritzer

MAKES 4 SERVINGS

- **3 bags hibiscus-lemon tea**
- **1½ cups boiling water**
- **⅓ cup sugar**
- **3 tablespoons lemon juice**
- **1½ cups pomegranate juice**
- **1 cup cold club soda**
- **4 lemon wedges**

1. Place tea bags in 2-cup heatproof measuring cup. Add boiling water; steep tea 5 minutes. Remove and discard tea bags; stir in sugar until dissolved. Cool to room temperature. Refrigerate until cold.
2. Combine tea, lemon juice and pomegranate juice in pitcher; mix well. Just before serving, stir in club soda. Serve over ice; garnish with lemon wedges.

Tropical Arnold Palmer

MAKES 4 SERVINGS

48 mint leaves (from 2 or 3 bunches of mint)

4 cups water, plus about 3 cups additional for filling ice trays

5 tropical fruit-flavored tea bags (such as passion fruit, peach or mango)

¾ cup frozen raspberry lemonade concentrate

1 lemon, cut into thin wedges

1. Place 2 mint leaves in each section of 2 ice cube trays (24 sections total). Fill with water and place in freezer until frozen.

2. Heat remaining 4 cups water in medium saucepan over medium-high heat until water begins to steam and barely simmer, about 4 minutes. Remove from heat; add tea bags and steep 3 minutes. Discard tea bags. Add frozen lemonade concentrate and stir until dissolved.

3. Place 12 mint ice cubes in pitcher. Pour tea mixture over ice; stir until ice melts.

4. Divide remaining mint ice cubes among four serving glasses; top with tea mixture. Garnish with lemon wedges.

Cardamom Lemonade Spritzer

MAKES 6 SERVINGS

- **3 cups water**
- **1¼ cups sugar**
- **40 whole white cardamom pods, cracked**
- **2 cups lemon juice**
- **1 bottle (2 liters) chilled club soda or lemon-lime soda**
- **Fresh mint leaves (optional)**

1. Combine water, sugar and cardamom pods in medium saucepan; bring to a simmer over high heat. Cook and stir until sugar dissolves. Reduce heat to low; cover and simmer 30 minutes. Remove from heat; cool completely. Refrigerate 2 hours or up to 3 days.

2. Pour mixture through strainer into large pitcher; stir in lemon juice and club soda. Serve over ice; garnish with mint leaves.

Grapefruit Slushy

MAKES 2 SERVINGS

3 tablespoons sugar, divided

1 to 2 drops red food coloring (optional)

1 grapefruit, peeled and seeded with membrane removed

1 cup ice cubes

¼ to ½ cup grapefruit juice

Fresh lavender or rosemary sprigs

1 Combine 1 tablespoon sugar and food coloring in small bowl, if desired; mix until evenly tinted. Moisten rims of two glasses; dip in red sugar.

2 Combine grapefruit, ice, grapefruit juice and remaining 2 tablespoons sugar in blender or food processor; blend until smooth.

3 Pour into prepared glasses. Garnish each serving with lavender sprigs; serve immediately.

Shirley Temple >

MAKES 1 SERVING

8 ounces chilled lemon-lime soda or ginger ale

1 ounce grenadine

Maraschino cherry

Fill highball glass half full with ice; top with soda and grenadine. Garnish with cherry.

Cuban Batido

MAKES 2 SERVINGS

1½ cups cubed fresh pineapple

6 ounces milk

4 ounces orange juice

3 tablespoons sugar

½ ounce lime juice

1 cup ice cubes

2 lime slices

1. Combine pineapple, milk, orange juice, sugar, lime juice and ice in blender; blend until smooth.

2. Pour into two glasses. Garnish with lime slices.

Almond Joyful Mocktini >

MAKES 2 SERVINGS

- **1 tablespoon dark chocolate syrup, plus additional for coating rims of glasses**
- **Shredded coconut**
- **6 ounces plain almond milk**
- **2 ounces vanilla coconut milk**

1 Coat rims of glasses with syrup; dip in coconut.

2 Fill cocktail shaker half full with ice; add milks and 1 tablespoon syrup. Shake 30 seconds or until very cold. Pour into prepared glasses.

Fuzz-less Navel

MAKES 1 SERVING

- **4 ounces peach mango juice**
- **2 ounces orange juice**
- **1 ounce lemon juice or lemonade**
- **Maraschino cherry**

Fill cocktail shaker half full with ice; add juices. Stir 30 seconds or until very cold. Strain into ice-filled glass; garnish with cherry.

Sleepytime Cocktail >

MAKES 1 SERVING

- **4 ounces tart cherry juice**
- **1 tablespoon magnesium powder**
- **Chilled lemon-lime prebiotic soda or sparkling water**

Fill cocktail shaker half full with ice; add juice and powder. Shake until well blended. Strain into ice-filled glass; top with soda.

Snowbird Mocktails

MAKES 10 SERVINGS

- **3 cups pineapple juice**
- **1 can (14 ounces) sweetened condensed milk**
- **½ (12-ounce) can frozen orange juice concentrate, thawed**
- **½ teaspoon coconut extract**
- **1 bottle (1 liter) chilled ginger ale**
- **Orange slices and maraschino cherries**

1. Combine pineapple juice, sweetened condensed milk, juice concentrate and coconut extract in large pitcher; stir well. Cover; refrigerate at least 1 hour or up to 1 week.

2. To serve, pour ½ cup pineapple juice mixture into glasses filled with crushed ice. Top each serving with about ⅓ cup ginger ale; garnish with orange slice and cherry.

Kiwi Lemonade >

MAKES 5 SERVINGS

- ¾ cup sugar
- 3 cups water, divided
- 8 ounces lemon juice
- 2 kiwis

1 Combine sugar and ½ cup water in small saucepan; cook over medium heat until sugar is dissolved. Remove from heat; cool slightly. Pour into pitcher. Add lemon juice and remaining 2½ cups water.

2 Peel kiwis and coarsely chop. Place in food processor; process until smooth. Strain into lemonade; stir until well blended. Refrigerate until cold.

NA Bellini

MAKES 1 SERVING

- 1 ounce peach nectar
- 2 ounces white grape juice
- 4 ounces chilled sparkling nonalcoholic apple cider

Pour peach nectar and grape juice into champagne flute; top with cider. Serve immediately.

Mango-Lime Virgin Margarita

MAKES 2 SERVINGS

- **2 lime wedges (optional)**
- **2 tablespoons coarse salt (optional)**
- **1 large ripe mango, peeled and cubed (1¼ to 1½ cups)**
- **1 cup ice**
- **½ cup lime juice**
- **⅓ cup water**
- **¼ cup sugar**
- **3 tablespoons orange juice**
- **Lime wedges (optional)**

1. Rub rims of two margarita glasses with lime wedges; dip in salt, if desired.

2. Combine mango, ice, lime juice, water, sugar and orange juice in blender; blend until smooth. Pour mixture into prepared glasses. Garnish with lime wedges.

Chilled Lemon Sunset

MAKES 4 SERVINGS

1½ cups water, divided
½ cup sugar
1 pint (2 cups) lemon sorbet
½ cup orange juice
¼ cup lemon juice
4 teaspoons grenadine
4 lemon slices

1. Combine ½ cup water and sugar in small saucepan; cook and stir over medium heat until sugar is dissolved. Transfer mixture to 2-cup glass measure. Cool to room temperature; refrigerate 1 hour.

2. Combine remaining 1 cup water, sugar syrup, sorbet, orange juice, and lemon juice in blender; blend until smooth.

3. Pour 1 teaspoon grenadine into bottom of each of four glasses; top with sorbet mixture. Garnish with lemon slices; serve immediately.

Piña Colada Shake >

MAKES 4 SERVINGS

2 cups (1 pint) coconut sorbet

2 cups (1 pint) vanilla frozen yogurt or ice cream

6 ounces pineapple juice

1 teaspoon rum extract (optional)

1 Combine sorbet, frozen yogurt, pineapple juice and rum extract, if desired, in blender. Process until smooth.

2 Pour into four glasses. Serve immediately.

Coconut Choco-tini

MAKES 4 SERVINGS

8 ounces cream of coconut

5 ounces chocolate syrup

8 ounces milk

1 teaspoon almond extract

3 cups ice cubes

Chocolate shavings

Combine cream of coconut, chocolate syrup, milk and almond extract in blender. Add ice; blend until smooth. Pour into cocktail glasses; garnish with chocolate shavings.

Ginger-Cucumber Limeade

MAKES 3 SERVINGS

- **1½ cups chopped seeded peeled cucumber**
- **⅓ cup frozen limeade concentrate, thawed**
- **1 teaspoon grated fresh ginger**
- **1 cup chilled club soda or sparkling water**
- **Cucumber slices and lime peel strips**

1 Combine chopped cucumber, limeade concentrate and ginger in blender; blend until smooth.

2 Combine cucumber mixture and club soda in small pitcher; gently stir. Serve over ice; garnish with cucumber slices and lime peel.

Raspberry Spritzer

MAKES 4 SERVINGS

1 bottle (1 liter) chilled seltzer water
1 cup frozen raspberries
6 ounces raspberry-flavored syrup
Lime wedges and fresh mint sprigs

1 Combine seltzer, raspberries and syrup in large pitcher; mix well.

2 Serve over ice; garnish with lime wedges and mint sprigs.

Tip

Fruit-flavored syrups are available at supermarkets and liquor stores. In addition to using them in mocktails and cocktails, you can also add them to coffee, tea, lattés, lemonade and smoothies for additional flavor.

Zero-Proof Party Drinks

Strawberry Lemonade

MAKES 5 SERVINGS

- **3 cups water, divided**
- **1 cup sugar**
- **1 cup frozen strawberries**
- **1½ cups lemon juice**

1 Combine 1 cup water, sugar and strawberries in small saucepan; bring to a boil over high heat. Boil 5 minutes. Remove from heat; cool completely.

2 Pour strawberry mixture into blender; blend until smooth. Strain into pitcher. Stir in lemon juice and remaining 2 cups water until blended. Refrigerate until cold.

Peach Iced Tea >

MAKES 4 SERVINGS

- **4 cups water**
- **3 black tea bags**
- **¼ cup sugar**
- **1 can (about 11 ounces) peach nectar**
- **1 cup frozen peach slices**

1. Bring water to a boil in medium saucepan over high heat. Remove from heat; add tea bags and let steep 5 minutes. Remove tea bags; stir in sugar until dissolved. Cool to room temperature.

2. Pour tea into pitcher. Stir in peach nectar and peach slices. Refrigerate until cold. Serve over ice.

Sunny Citrus Float

MAKES 4 SERVINGS

- **4 cups cold water**
- **½ cup sweetened lemon-flavored iced tea mix**
- **⅓ cup frozen lemonade concentrate, thawed**
- **⅓ cup frozen orange juice concentrate, thawed**
- **1 cup vanilla frozen yogurt or ice cream**

Combine water, tea mix, lemonade concentrate and orange juice concentrate in large pitcher. Pour tea mixture into four glasses; top each with ¼ cup frozen yogurt.

Raspberry Lemonade Slushies >

MAKES 6 SERVINGS

- 1½ cups fresh or frozen raspberries
- 1 can (6 ounces) frozen lemonade concentrate
- 1 cup water
- 4 cups ice cubes

1. Combine raspberries, lemonade concentrate and water in blender or food processor; blend until smooth. Add ice; blend until smooth.
2. Pour into six glasses; serve immediately.

Guava Fruit Punch

MAKES 4 SERVINGS

- 1½ cups boiling water
- 2 decaffeinated tea bags
- 3 thin slices peeled fresh ginger
- 2 cups guava juice
- ¾ cup pineapple juice
- 1 to 2 tablespoons lemon juice

1. Combine boiling water, tea bags and ginger in heatproof pitcher; steep 5 minutes. Discard tea bags and ginger. Cool to room temperature.
2. Add guava juice, pineapple juice and lemon juice to tea mixture; mix well. Serve over ice.

Cucumber Punch >

MAKES ABOUT 5 SERVINGS

- **1 seedless cucumber, thinly sliced**
- **1 cup water**
- **½ (12-ounce) can thawed frozen limeade concentrate**
- **1 bottle (1 liter) chilled club soda**
- **Lime wedges**

1. Combine cucumber slices, water and limeade concentrate in punch bowl or pitcher. Refrigerate 1 hour.
2. Add club soda just before serving. Serve over ice; garnish with lime wedges.

Strawberry-Mango Daiquiri Punch

MAKES 8 SERVINGS

- **3 cups cubed fresh mango**
- **3 cups frozen strawberries**
- **1 can (12 ounces) frozen limeade concentrate, thawed**
- **¾ cup pineapple juice**
- **2½ cups chilled lemon-lime soda**

1. Combine mango, strawberries, limeade and pineapple juice in blender. Blend until nearly smooth. Pour into pitcher.
2. Gently stir in soda; serve over ice.

Strawberry-Basil Sparklers

MAKES ABOUT 8 SERVINGS

- **1 cup fresh basil leaves, plus additional for serving**
- **⅔ cup sugar**
- **⅔ cup water**
- **4 cups fresh strawberries, plus additional for garnish**
- **1 bottle (2 liters) chilled club soda**

1 Combine 1 cup basil, sugar and water in small saucepan; cook and stir over medium heat until sugar is dissolved. Remove from heat; cool completely. Strain through fine-mesh sieve into blender; discard basil. (Syrup can be made ahead and stored in refrigerator up to 1 week.)

2 Add 4 cups strawberries to blender; blend until smooth. Pour into pitcher; stir in club soda just before serving. Serve over ice; garnish with additional strawberries and basil.

Cherry Limeade >

MAKES 8 SERVINGS

- 4 limes
- 1 bottle (2 liters) chilled lemon-lime soda
- 1 can (12 ounces) frozen limeade concentrate
- 1 jar (16 ounces) stemmed maraschino cherries
- Lime wedges

Juice 4 limes into large pitcher. Add soda, limeade and cherries with juice; stir gently. Serve over ice; garnish with lime wedges.

Citrus Cooler

MAKES 8 SERVINGS

- 2 cups orange juice
- 2 cups pineapple juice
- ¼ cup lemon juice
- ¾ teaspoon coconut extract
- ¾ teaspoon vanilla
- 2 cups chilled sparkling water
- Ice cubes

1. Combine orange juice, pineapple juice, lemon juice, coconut extract and vanilla in large pitcher; refrigerate until cold.
2. Stir in sparkling water just before serving. Serve over ice.

Razzle Dazzle Apple-Berry Punch

MAKES 10 SERVINGS

8 to 12 medium fresh strawberries *or* 30 fresh red raspberries

7 cups apple juice, divided

1 (4-inch) cinnamon stick, broken

½ teaspoon whole allspice

½ teaspoon vanilla

2 cans (12 ounces each) chilled lemon-lime soda or ginger ale

1. Cut strawberries in half. Place one strawberry half in each section of three ice cube trays. Spoon about 1 tablespoon of apple juice over each piece of fruit. Freeze until firm.

2. Combine remaining apple juice, cinnamon stick and allspice in large saucepan; bring to a boil. Reduce heat; cover and simmer 5 minutes. Remove from heat; stir in vanilla. Cover and refrigerate 6 hours or until cold.

3. Strain apple juice through fine-mesh strainer into pitcher or small punch bowl. Gently stir in soda. Add frozen apple juice cubes.

Bubbling Raspberry Coolers

MAKES 8 TO 10 SERVINGS

- **¾ cup raspberry vinegar**
- **½ cup sugar**
- **1 bottle (2 liters) chilled seltzer water**
- **2 cups fresh raspberries**
- **Fresh mint leaves**

1. Combine raspberry vinegar and sugar in small saucepan; bring to a boil over medium heat. Boil 1 minute or until sugar is dissolved, stirring frequently. Cool completely.

2. Pour cooled syrup into large pitcher; stir in seltzer water. To serve, fill each glass with ice, ¼ cup raspberries and mint leaves. Fill glasses with seltzer mixture. Serve immediately.

Lime-Apple Green Tea Spritzer

MAKES 6 SERVINGS

2 green tea bags
4 cups boiling water
¼ cup plus 1 tablespoon sugar
2 cups chilled apple juice
2 cups chilled seltzer
¼ cup lime juice
Green apple slices (optional)

1 Place tea bags in 4-cup heatproof measuring cup. Add boiling water; steep tea 5 minutes. Remove and discard tea bags; stir in sugar until dissolved. Refrigerate until cold.

2 Pour tea into pitcher. Stir in apple juice, seltzer and lime juice. Serve over ice; garnish with apple slices.

Ginger and Apple Spritzer

MAKES 4 TO 6 SERVINGS

- **3 English breakfast tea bags**
- **1 cup boiling water**
- **¼ cup sugar**
- **2 tablespoons minced crystallized ginger**
- **2 tablespoons lemon juice**
- **3 cups chilled sparkling nonalcoholic apple cider**
- **4 to 6 lemon wedges**

1. Place tea bags in 2-cup heatproof measuring cup. Add boiling water; steep tea 5 minutes. Remove and discard tea bags; stir in sugar until dissolved. Refrigerate until cold.

2. Combine tea, ginger and lemon juice in pitcher; mix well. (This can be done several hours in advance; refrigerate until ready to serve.)

3. Just before serving, stir in sparkling cider. Serve over ice; garnish with lemon wedges.

Citrus Punch

MAKES 8 TO 10 SERVINGS

4 oranges, sectioned
1 pint fresh strawberries, stemmed and halved
1 to 2 limes, cut into ⅛-inch slices
1 lemon, cut into ⅛-inch slices
1 cup fresh raspberries
2 cups orange juice
2 cups grapefruit juice
¾ cup lime juice
½ cup light corn syrup
1 bottle (2 liters) chilled ginger ale or lemon-lime soda

1 Spread orange sections, strawberries, lime slices, lemon slices and raspberries on baking sheet. Freeze 4 hours or until firm.

2 Combine juices and corn syrup in large pitcher; stir until corn syrup dissolves. Refrigerate 2 hours or until cold. Stir in ginger ale just before serving.

3 Divide frozen fruit among 8 (12-ounce) glasses or 10 wide-rimmed wine glasses. Fill glasses with punch; serve immediately.

Strawberry-Apricot Punch

MAKES 12 SERVINGS

- **2 packages (10 ounces each) frozen sliced strawberries in syrup, thawed**
- **2 cans (5½ ounces each) apricot or peach nectar**
- **¼ cup lemon juice**
- **2 tablespoons honey**
- **1 bottle (2 liters) chilled lemon-lime soda**
- **Lemon slices or fresh strawberry halves (optional)**

1. Place strawberries with syrup in food processor or blender; process until smooth.

2. Pour puréed strawberries into large punch bowl. Stir in apricot nectar, lemon juice and honey until well blended.

3. To serve, stir soda into strawberry mixture. Float lemon slices and fresh strawberries.

Spiced Piña Colada Punch

MAKES 12 SERVINGS

- **3 cups water**
- **10 whole cloves**
- **4 cardamom pods**
- **2 cinnamon sticks**
- **1 pint piña colada frozen yogurt, softened***
- **1 can (12 ounces) frozen pineapple juice concentrate, thawed**
- **1¼ cups chilled lemon seltzer water**
- **1¼ teaspoons rum extract**
- **¾ teaspoon coconut extract (optional)**

Or substitute pineapple sherbet and use the optional coconut extract.

1. Combine water, cloves, cardamom and cinnamon in small saucepan; bring to a boil over high heat. Reduce heat to low; cover and simmer 5 minutes. Cool to room temperature. Strain syrup through fine-mesh strainer into small punch bowl or pitcher.

2. Add frozen yogurt and juice concentrate to pitcher; stir until frozen yogurt is melted. Stir in seltzer water, rum extract and coconut extract, if desired.

Sparkling Tropical Fruit Combo

MAKES 3 SERVINGS

- ¾ cup chilled orange-tangerine juice or orange juice
- ¾ cup chilled passion fruit juice or guava-pineapple juice
- ¾ cup chilled club soda or sparkling water
- Lime slices and maraschino cherries

1. Combine orange-tangerine juice and passion fruit juice in pitcher. Gently stir in club soda.
2. Serve over ice; garnish with lime slices and cherries.

Healthy Elixirs

Melonade

MAKES 4 SERVINGS

- **¼ seedless watermelon, rind removed**
- **1 apple**
- **1 lemon, peeled**

Juice watermelon, apple and lemon. Stir.

Sharp Apple Cooler >

MAKES 3 SERVINGS

- **3 apples**
- **1 cucumber**
- **¼ cup fresh mint**
- **1 inch fresh ginger, peeled**

Juice apples, cucumber, mint and ginger. Stir.

Grape Berry Smoothie

MAKES 3 SERVINGS

- **½ cup water**
- **2 cups seedless red grapes**
- **2 cups frozen blackberries**
- **2 cups baby spinach**
- **½ cup ice cubes**
- **¼ teaspoon ground cinnamon**

Combine water, grapes, blackberries, spinach, ice and cinnamon in blender; blend until smooth. Serve immediately.

Orchard Crush Juice >

MAKES 2 SERVINGS

2 apples

1 cup fresh raspberries

1 cup fresh strawberries

Juice apples, raspberries and strawberries. Stir.

Strawberry Apple Smoothie

MAKES 2 SERVINGS

¾ cup water

1 sweet red apple, seeded and cut into chunks

1 clementine, peeled

1 cup frozen strawberries

1 tablespoon lemon juice

Combine water, apple, clementine, strawberries and lemon juice in blender; blend until smooth. Serve immediately.

Cucumber Basil Cooler >

MAKES 2 SERVINGS

- **1 cucumber**
- **1 apple**
- **½ cup fresh basil**
- **½ lime, peeled**

Juice cucumber, apple, basil and lime. Stir.

Vitamin C Blast

MAKES 3 SERVINGS

- **⅔ cup water**
- **2 navel oranges, peeled and seeded**
- **2 cups frozen blackberries**
- **2 cups baby kale**
- **1 avocado**
- **2 tablespoons honey**

Combine water, oranges, blackberries, kale, avocado and honey in blender; blend until smooth. Serve immediately.

Sweet Pepper Carrot Juice >

MAKES 2 SERVINGS

3 carrots
1 red bell pepper
1 yellow bell pepper

Juice carrots and bell peppers. Stir.

Refreshing Green Smoothie

MAKES 1 SERVING

1 cup baby spinach
¾ cup frozen pineapple chunks
¾ cup coconut milk
½ teaspoon grated lemon peel

Combine spinach, pineapple, coconut milk and lemon peel in blender; blend until smooth. Serve immediately.

Super C Juice >

MAKES 3 SERVINGS

- **2 oranges, peeled**
- **1 grapefruit, peeled**
- **1 lemon, peeled**
- **½ cup fresh cranberries**
- **2 teaspoons honey**

Juice oranges, grapefruit, lemon and cranberries. Stir in honey until blended.

Double Green Pineapple Juice

MAKES 1 SERVING

- **4 leaves Swiss chard**
- **4 leaves kale**
- **¼ pineapple, peeled**

Juice chard, kale and pineapple. Stir.

Triple Green Smoothie >

MAKES 2 SERVINGS

2 cups seedless green grapes
1 kiwi, peeled and quartered
½ avocado

Combine grapes, kiwi and avocado in blender; blend until smooth. Serve immediately.

Tropical Smoothie

MAKES 2 SERVINGS

¼ cup water
1 cup peeled papaya chunks
1 cup frozen pineapple chunks
½ frozen banana
1 tablespoon lemon juice
⅛ teaspoon ground cinnamon

Combine water, papaya, pineapple, banana, lemon juice and cinnamon in blender; blend until smooth.

Cherry Green Smoothie >

MAKES 2 SERVINGS

- **¾ cup almond milk**
- **1½ cups frozen dark sweet cherries**
- **¾ cup baby spinach**
- **½ frozen banana**
- **1 tablespoon ground flaxseed**
- **2 teaspoons honey (optional)**

Combine almond milk, cherries, spinach, banana, flaxseed and honey, if desired, in blender; blend until smooth. Serve immediately.

Fiery Cucumber Beet Juice

MAKES 2 SERVINGS

- **1 cucumber**
- **1 beet**
- **1 lemon, peeled**
- **1 inch fresh ginger, peeled**
- **½ jalapeño pepper**

Juice cucumber, beet, lemon, ginger and jalapeño pepper. Stir.

Cran-Orange Raspberry Smoothie >

MAKES 2 SERVINGS

- **¼ cup water**
- **2 navel oranges, peeled and seeded**
- **½ cup fresh or thawed frozen cranberries**
- **½ cup frozen raspberries**
- **2 teaspoons honey**

Combine water, oranges, cranberries, raspberries and honey in blender; blend until smooth. Serve immediately.

Immunity Booster Juice

MAKES 3 SERVINGS

- **1 grapefruit, peeled**
- **2 oranges, peeled**
- **½ cup fresh blackberries**

Juice grapefruit, oranges and blackberries. Stir.

Grape Cherry Smoothie >

MAKES 2 SERVINGS

1 cup seedless red grapes

1 navel orange, peeled and seeded

½ cup frozen dark sweet cherries

¼ cup ice cubes

Combine grapes, orange, cherries and ice in blender; blend until smooth. Serve immediately.

Cherry Melon Juice

MAKES 3 SERVINGS

⅛ small watermelon, rind removed

¼ cantaloupe, rind removed

¾ cup cherries, pitted

Juice watermelon, cantaloupe and cherries. Stir.

Conversion Chart

¼ ounce	=	½ tablespoon
½ ounce	=	1 tablespoon
¾ ounce	=	1½ tablespoons
1 ounce	=	2 tablespoons
2 ounces	=	¼ cup
4 ounces	=	½ cup
6 ounces	=	¾ cup
8 ounces	=	1 cup
16 ounces	=	2 cups
24 ounces	=	3 cups
32 ounces	=	1 quart

Volume Equivalents (Liquid)

US STANDARD	US STANDARD (OUNCES)	METRIC (APPROXIMATE)
2 tablespoons	1 fluid ounce	30 mL
½ cup	4 fluid ounces	125 mL
1 cup	8 fluid ounces	250 mL
1 ½ cups	12 fluid ounces	375 mL
2 cups	16 fluid ounces	500 mL